A is for Arrow

A SCULPTURE IS NOT ALWAYS SOMETHING YOU CAN RECOGNIZE. **T**HIS KIND OF SCULPTURE IS CALLED ABSTRACT.

Obus/Alexander Calder/1972
National Gallery of Art, Washington, D.C.

3

B

SOMETIMES A
SCULPTURE IS MADE
OF THINGS THAT
ALREADY EXIST.
THIS IS CALLED A
READY-MADE.

BICYCLE WHEEL
MARCEL DUCHAMP/1913
THE VERA AND ARTURO
SCHWARZ COLLECTION OF
DADA AND SURREALIST ART,
THE ISRAEL MUSEUM,
JERUSALEM, ISRAEL

3-D ABC

A SCULPTURAL ALPHABET

by Bob Raczka

M MILLBROOK PRESS/MINNEAPOLIS

TO MY MY THREE "B" BROTHERS
(BILL, BRIAN, AND BRAD)

Text copyright © 2007 by Bob Raczka

Artwork copyright notices on page 32.

Millbrook Press, Inc.
A division of Lerner Publishing Group, Inc.
241 First Avenue North
Minneapolis, Minnesota 55401 U.S.A.

Website address: www.lernerbooks.com

Library of Congress Cataloging-in-Publication Data

Raczka, Bob.
3-D ABC : a sculptural
alphabet / by Bob Raczka.
p. cm.
ISBN-13: 978-0-7613-9456-3 (lib. bdg. : alk. paper)
ISBN-10: 0-7613-9456-7 (lib. bdg. : alk. paper)
1. Sculpture—Juvenile literature.
2. Alphabet books—Juvenile literature. I. Title.
NB1143.R33 2007
730—dc22   2005013472

Manufactured in the United States of America
3 4 5 6 7 8 - JR - 12 11 10 09 08 07

A SCULPTURE MIGHT BE SOMETHING YOU
RECOGNIZE, LIKE A CAR, BUT MADE OUT
OF SOMETHING UNEXPECTED, LIKE WOOD.

YOU ARE DRIVING A VOLVO/JULIAN OPIE/1996
LISSON GALLERY, LONDON, ENGLAND

ALL SCULPTURES ARE THREE-
DIMENSIONAL. MOST CAN BE
LOOKED AT FROM ALL SIDES.

TANGO/ELIE
NADELMAN/ CA. 1920–1924
WHITNEY MUSEUM OF
AMERICAN ART,
NEW YORK, NEW YORK

THIS SCULPTURE CAN BE LOOKED AT FROM JUST ONE SIDE. IT'S CALLED A RELIEF.

CARVED AMERICAN EAGLE
JOHN BELLAMY/1880
HYLAND GRANBY ANTIQUES,
HYANNIS PORT,
MASSACHUSETTS

SOME SCULPTURES ARE
AT HOME OUTDOORS.

FAMILY GROUP
HENRY MOORE
1948–1949
HENRY MOORE
FOUNDATION,
PERRY GREEN,
HERTFORDSHIRE,
ENGLAND

Some outdoor sculptures are so big, you can walk right under them. Or they can walk right over you.

WALKING MAN/Jonathan Borofsky/1994–1995
Munich Re headquarters, Munich, Germany

9

H

H is for Horse

A SCULPTURE CAN BE

PIECES OF SCRAP METAL

THAT THE SCULPTOR

FINDS AND FORMS INTO

A FAMILIAR-LOOKING

SHAPE . . .

Ikezuke/Deborah Butterfield/1994
Greg Kucera Gallery, Seattle, Washington

I is for Instrument

. . . OR

A FAMILIAR-SOUNDING SHAPE.

Guitar/Pablo Picasso/1912–1913
Museum of Modern Art,
New York, New York

J is for Junk

Dolores James
John Chamberlain
1962
Solomon R.
Guggenheim Museum,
New York, New York

EVEN THE PIECES OF SOMETHING THAT WAS

WRECKED CAN BE TURNED INTO A SCULPTURE.

K is for Kiss

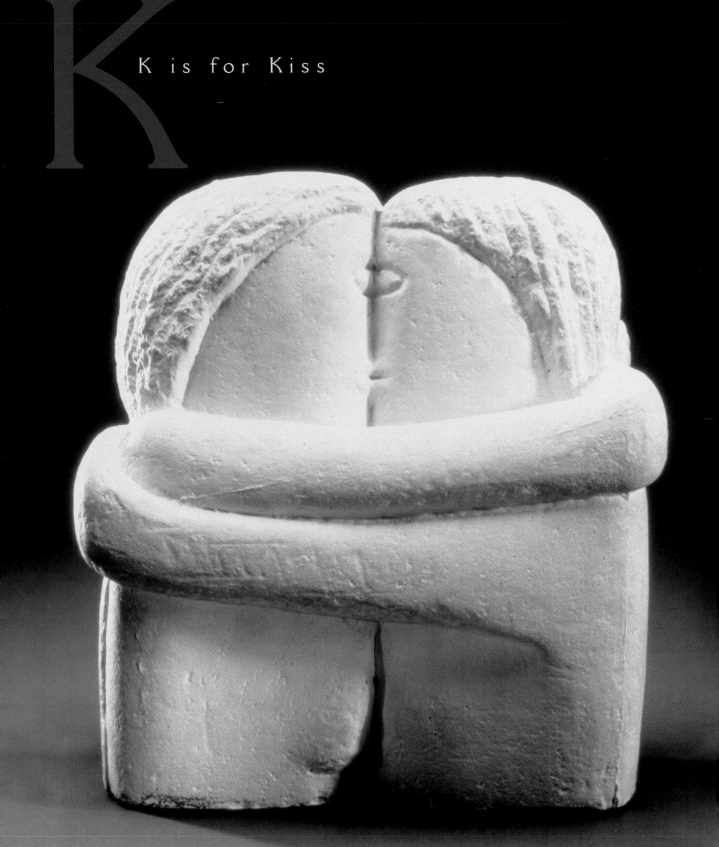

SOMETIMES, TWO COMPLETELY DIFFERENT SCULPTURES . . .

THE KISS/CONSTANTIN BRANCUSI/1908–1909, PRIVATE COLLECTION

Love
ROBERT INDIANA/1966
BRIGHAM YOUNG UNIVERSITY
MUSEUM OF ART, PROVO,
UTAH

. . . CAN SAY EXACTLY THE SAME THING.

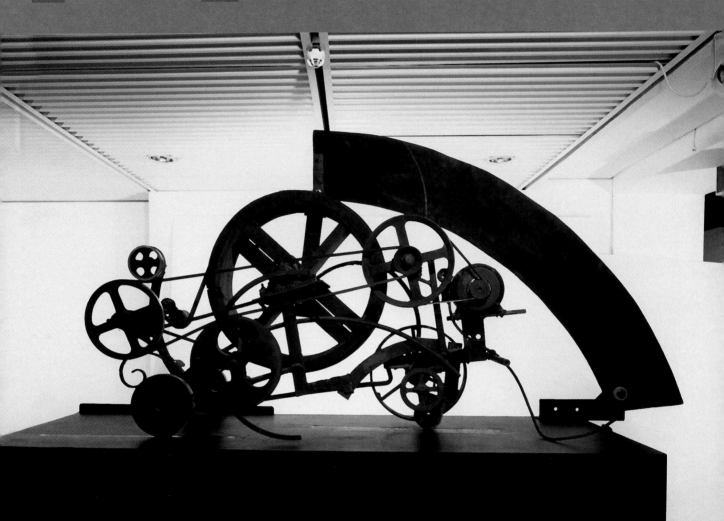

A SCULPTURE CAN HAVE MOVING PARTS.

THIS IS CALLED KINETIC SCULPTURE.

CHARIOT MK IV/JEAN TINGUELY/1966
MODERNA MUSEET, STOCKHOLM, SWEDEN

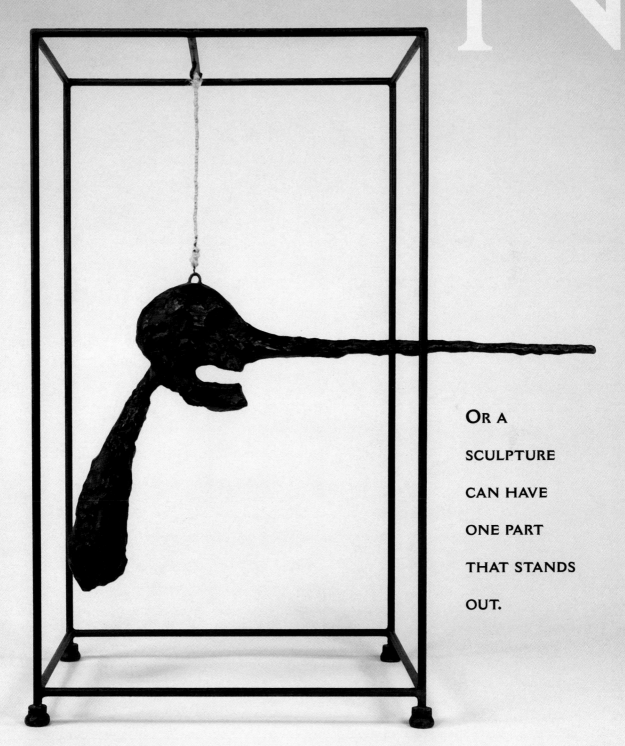

OR A
SCULPTURE
CAN HAVE
ONE PART
THAT STANDS
OUT.

Nose
ALBERTO GIACOMETTI
1947
SOLOMON R. GUGGENHEIM MUSEUM,
NEW YORK, NEW YORK

O is for Obelisk

P is for Pyramid

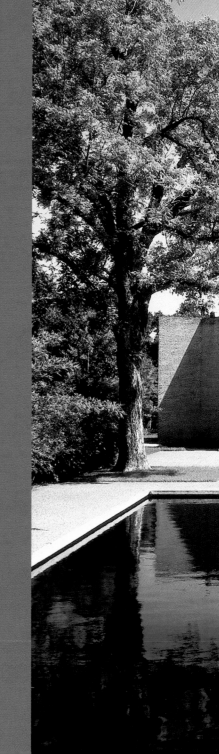

SOME SCULPTURES LOOK IMPOSSIBLE.

Broken Obelisk
Barnett
Newman
1963–1967
Rothko
Chapel,
Houston

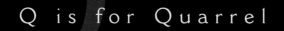

Q is for Quarrel

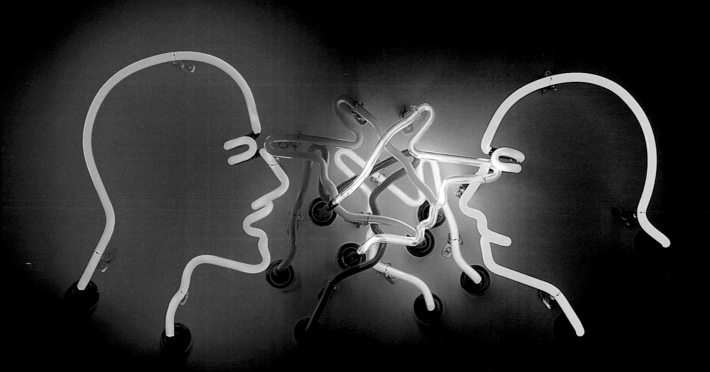

A SCULPTURE CAN BE MADE OUT OF LIGHT.

DOUBLE POKE IN THE EYE II/BRUCE NAUMAN/1985
KEMPER MUSEUM OF CONTEMPORARY ART, KANSAS CITY, MISSOURI

OR IT CAN MAKE YOU SEE

SOMETHING THAT ISN'T THERE.

BUS RIDERS
GEORGE SEGAL/1964
HIRSHHORN MUSEUM AND SCULPTURE GARDEN,
WASHINGTON, D.C.

S is for Spoon

A SCULPTURE CAN MAKE YOU SMILE

SPOONBRIDGE AND CHERRY/CLAES OLDENBURG
AND COOSJE VAN BRUGGEN/1985–1988
WALKER ART CENTER, MINNEAPOLIS, MINNESOTA

T is for Tablecloth

OR MAKE YOU THINK

ABOUT DINNER.

TABLE WITH PINK TABLECLOTH
RICHARD ARTSCHWAGER/1964
THE ART INSTITUTE OF CHICAGO,
CHICAGO, ILLINOIS

U is for Upside Down

A SCULPTURE CAN MAKE YOU

LOOK AT THINGS DIFFERENTLY,

CONCERT FOR ANARCHY/REBECCA HORN/1990
TATE GALLERY, LONDON, ENGLAND

EVEN

THINGS YOU

SEE EVERY

DAY.

New Hoover Celebrity III/Jeff Koons/1980
Museum of Contemporary Art, Los Angeles, California

A Case for an Angel II
Antony Gormley
1990
Contemporary Sculpture Center
Tokyo, Japan

W is for Wings

A SCULPTURE CAN
HELP YOUR
IMAGINATION SOAR.

A SCULPTURE CAN MEAN DIFFERENT THINGS TO DIFFERENT PEOPLE,

THE X
RONALD BLADEN/1967
MIAMI-DADE ART IN
PUBLIC PLACES,
MIAMI, FLORIDA

28

OR IT CAN MEAN DIFFERENT THINGS TO THE SAME PERSON ON DIFFERENT DAYS,

MIDDAY/ANTHONY CARO/1960
MUSEUM OF MODERN ART,
NEW YORK, NEW YORK

29

Z

BECAUSE THE
MORE YOU
LOOK AT A
SCULPTURE,
THE MORE
YOU SEE.

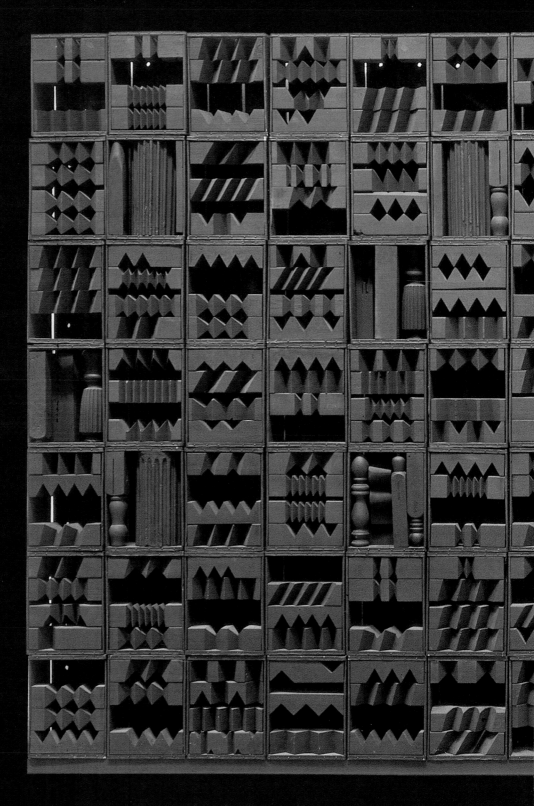

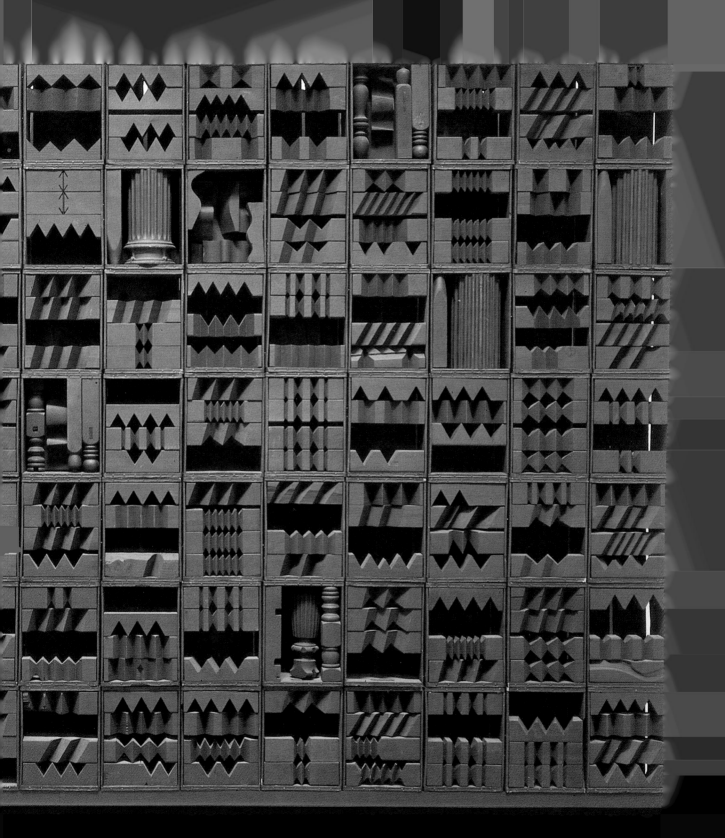

Photo Credit